Dear Parent:
Your child's love of reading starts here!

Every child learns to read in a different way and at his or her own speed. Some go back and forth between reading levels and read favorite books again and again. Others read through each level in order. You can help your young reader improve and become more confident by encouraging his or her own interests and abilities. From books your child reads with you to the first books he or she reads alone, there are I Can Read Books for every stage of reading:

SHARED READING
Basic language, word repetition, and whimsical illustrations, ideal for sharing with your emergent reader

BEGINNING READING
Short sentences, familiar words, and simple concepts for children eager to read on their own

READING WITH HELP
Engaging stories, longer sentences, and language play for developing readers

READING ALONE
Complex plots, challenging vocabulary, and high-interest topics for the independent reader

ADVANCED READING
Short paragraphs, chapters, and exciting themes for the perfect bridge to chapter books

I Can Read Books have introduced children to the joy of reading since 1957. Featuring award-winning authors and illustrators and a fabulous cast of beloved characters, I Can Read Books set the standard for beginning readers.

A lifetime of discovery begins with the magical words "I Can Read!"

Visit www.icanread.com for information
on enriching your child's reading experience.

To my own family pack: Samson, Sophia, Rita, and Chris
—J.B.

The author would like to thank David Mizejewski, the naturalist at the
National Wildlife Federation, for his guidance and expertise.

The National Wildlife Federation and Ranger Rick contributors: Children's
Publication and Licensing Staff.

Ranger Rick: I Wish I Was a Wolf
Copyright © 2019 National Wildlife Federation. All rights reserved.
Manufactured in China. No part of this book may be used or reproduced in any manner whatsoever without
written permission except in the case of brief quotations embodied in critical articles and reviews. For
information address HarperCollins Children's Books, a division of HarperCollins Publishers, 195 Broadway,
New York, NY 10007.
www.icanread.com
www.RangerRick.com

Library of Congress Control Number: 2018943095
ISBN 978-0-06-243220-9 (trade bdg.)—ISBN 978-0-06-243219-3 (pbk.)

Typography by Brenda E. Angelilli
18 19 20 21 22 SCP 10 9 8 7 6 5 4 3 2 1 ❖ First Edition

RANGER RICK
NATIONAL WILDLIFE FEDERATION

Ranger Rick

I Wish I Was a Wolf

by Jennifer Bové

HARPER
An Imprint of HarperCollinsPublishers

What if you wished you were a wolf?

Then you became a wolf pup.

Could you play like a pup?

Talk with howls and growls?

Grow up in a wolf family?

And would you want to? Find out!

Where would you live?

Wolves live all over the northern part of the world. They can be found in forests, grasslands, and mountains. They even live in the cold Arctic, near the North Pole.

Would you like to live here?

Wolves look like big dogs.

They act like dogs, too.

That's because they are dogs:

wild dogs.

Wolves don't live in houses.

Wolves live far from people

with their own wolf families.

What would your family be like?

A wolf family is called a pack.

The pack has a mother, a father,

and wolf kids, called pups.

Young adults help take care of their little brothers and sisters.

A big brother or sister plays with the young pups and watches for danger while the rest of the pack goes hunting for food.

How would you learn to be a wolf?

Wolf pups watch adult wolves
and copy what they do.
Pups practice hunting
by playing with each other.
They chase and wrestle.
They will use these skills
to hunt animals for food.

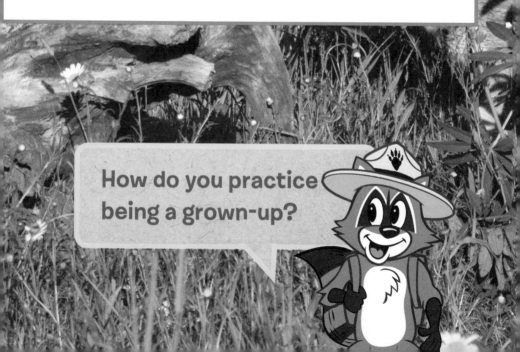

How do you practice
being a grown-up?

What would you eat?

Wolves eat meat from deer, elk, caribou, moose, and bison. Wolf packs work together to hunt these large animals.

Adult wolves eat lots of meat.
Then the adults throw up mushy meat
for the young pups to eat.
Thrown-up meat is easy for pups
to chew with their little teeth.

Would you want to eat mushy meat?

How would you wash up?

Like all dogs, wolves wash up
by licking their own fur.
Mother wolves lick their pups
until they are big enough
to bathe themselves.

How would you talk?

When wolves have something to say
they lift their noses and HOWL!
A wolf pack howls together to say,
"We're a great team!"
When wolves are apart
they howl to tell others,
"I'm over here!"
Howls can be heard for many miles.

Wolves make other sounds, too.

A bark means, "Watch out!"

Whimpering means,

"Let's be friends."

Adult wolves growl to say,
"Back off!"
But pups growl for fun
when they play.

Wolves talk with their bodies, too.

A wolf shows its teeth to say,

"Leave me alone."

Wolves say hi by wagging tails,

sniffing, and rolling upside down.

How would growing up change you?

Pups begin hunting with the pack when they are six months old. By age three, wolves are full grown.

When they grow up,
many wolves leave their parents
to find mates from other packs.
These wolves start new packs
with pups of their own.

Would you like to grow up that fast?

Being a wolf could be cool

for a while.

But do you want to live outdoors?

Lick yourself clean?

Eat thrown-up meat?

Luckily, you don't have to.

You're not a wolf.

You're YOU!

Did You Know?

- A large adult wolf can weigh up to 175 pounds (79 kilograms).

- A wolf's fur can be gray, but it can also be black, white, or brown.

- Wolf howls can be heard from 10 miles (16 kilometers) away.

- Wolves can run as fast as 40 miles (64 kilometers) per hour.

- The average life span of a wolf in the wild is six to eight years.

Fun Zone

Wolves make many sounds to talk to each other. Their sounds have different meanings, almost like human words. Can you talk like a wolf?
Try this activity with a friend—or a whole pack of friends—to find out.

🐾 Listen to real wolf sounds on this website: www.livingwithwolves.org/about-wolves/language/#vocal

🐾 Practice making these wolf sounds:
- **•Howl**   **•Growl**
- **•Whimper** **•Bark**

🐾 Try talking to friends with these sounds. Can you understand each other?

🐾 Now that you and your pack can talk like wolves, try playing a game of tag or hide-and-seek using only wolf sounds.

Wild Words

Arctic: land near the North Pole that is cold, dry, and snowy most of the year

Howl: a loud, long call made by wolves to talk over long distances

Hunt: to chase and catch animals to eat

Pack: a family of wolves

Pup: a young wolf

Dig Deeper
WANT TO FIND OUT EVEN MORE ABOUT WOLVES?
Check out the Ranger Rick website: www.RangerRick.com
SEARCH: wolves

Photography © Getty Images: by JohnPitcher, JudiLen, Lynn_Bystrom, dssimages, KenCanning, labrlo, Jim Cumming, porsche99, Adria Photography, Tom Brakefield, jimkruger, BlackAperture, twildlife, gnagel, Reemow, karlumbriacod